SILHOUETTES OF THE
BIG FOUR

R.J. BLENKINSOP

© Oxford Publishing Co. 1980
SBN 90 2888 78 1
Typesetting by Katerprint Co. Ltd., Oxford
Lithographic Reproduction by Knight Publishing Ltd., Oxford
Printed by Blackwell's in the City of Oxford

Published by
Oxford Publishing Co.
8 The Roundway
Headington
Oxford

PREFACE

Although steam traction on British Rail was to continue for another three years after the last pictures in this book were taken, the run down was sad and only here and there was any attempt made to keep up appearances. To the enthusiast the sight and sound of the steam railway was paramount and the breeding diesels, with speed and efficiency, soon reduced the steam locomotive population to a few hundred.

Even before these days of rocketing fuel costs for the motor car, it was not cheap to travel several hundred miles in a day just to obtain a handful of pictures covering the last of a class wheezing out its days on some downgraded freight train.

This thinking becomes apparent in this book where, although I always carried my Leica with me, the location became repetitive as many were the result of some business appointment. However holidays fortunately were spent in the Isle of Wight and this was still steam operated together with the Southern main line through Southampton where I managed to obtain the odd day out away from digging sand castles on the beach. You can perhaps imagine the frustration of sitting in the sun on the beach and dreaming of all those splendid Pacifics still in their prime and working such beautiful trains as the *Bournemouth Belle* and out of camera reach!

The London terminals were interesting and particularly Kings Cross where the A4s were still kept clean and they were rubbing shoulders with the new Deltics. Also of course there was no sign of electrification on the East Coast main line but things were different farther west.

London Midland were in the throes of the enormous Crewe to Euston project and many trains were being diverted on Sundays. My local line through the village became a main line on Sundays and every conceivable express type of L.M.S. locomotive appeared at some time or other. You will find a picture of a 'Princess' Class passing Leamington Spa Avenue Station, a working quite unheard of until the 1960's.

At this time there were many 'last trains' run by the railway societies and the Stephenson Locomotive Society in particular. I tried to travel on most of the ones which started from Birmingham and they feature in the book. Quite a number of the locomotives have survived into preservation and hopefully will continue to operate for quite a number of years to come.

Locomotives picking up water have always been a favourite subject of mine for the camera and the picture No. 27 is of interest, taken on the West Coast main line and before the electricity was switched on. Whenever I look at this picture I think of the guard about to put his head out of that open window at just the moment the tender overflowed!

Looking at the number of locomotive spotters shown in some of the pictures I remember thinking at the time what it would be like when the steam engine had gone and if the interest in diesels would take their place. I am sure it has and judging by the number of people taking numbers on the main stations today I do not think it matters one bit what is the form of motive power at the front end.

One of the most exciting 'last trains' I travelled on was the Birmingham to Swindon outing with **King Henry VI** shown in pictures 61 and 62. All the class had been withdrawn during the winter and No. 6018 so the story goes, had been earmarked for preservation at one of the Butlin Holiday Camps. In fact nothing came of this and the engine spent some time languishing at Swindon Works before being allowed to run again in April 1963. The previous week it had been running between Tyseley and Leamington Spa on a local evening train and while being turned on the turntable a 'Duchess' went by just a few yards away on the Midland line from Rugby. Alas, it came without warning and it was not possible to grab a picture of the most powerful engines from the L.M.S. and G.W.R.

On arriving at Swindon the 'King' went on shed and simmered in the Spring sunshine for all to photograph surrounded by 'Hymek' diesels all of which have also gone to the breakers yard. For the final trip of G.W. engines from Birmingham the locomotive number on the smokebox was always removed and transfers applied to the buffer beam, together with the shed code TYS painted as shown just below the lamp. The object of course was to make the locomotive as near G.W. as possible but with a double chimney then fitted it did not really have much effect!

This is the last book in the series of the Big Four, all the volumes covering a period of some 14 years of railway photography. The challenge today for the photographer of the modern scene is greater due to standardisation of trains throughout the system and the difficult interpretation of a machine which in the picture gives little feel as to whether it is in motion. However the quality of cameras that can be purchased by almost anyone is quite superb and there is little excuse for even the novice to fail to obtain good results.

1 A dull July morning sees No 6016 **King Edward** V passing Old Oak Common and taking the Birmingham route, through Bicester, with the *Inter-City*. On the right is a pannier tank with a local freight waiting for the road.

26th July 1961

△

2 Stanier 8F No 48142 crosses the Western Region main line near North Acton with a transfer freight for the Midland Region.
26th July 1961

3 Taken from the same location an unusual picture of V2 No 60879 climbing to join the Western Region with a train that it has most probably taken over at Kensington Olympia. This double track has now been lifted and the London Transport lines in the foreground are part of the Central Line.
26th July 1961

WEST RUISLIP

4   Here we are looking south with Wormwood Scrubs Prison behind 'Britannia' Pacific No 70016 **Ariel** awaiting signals with a parcels train for Paddington. In the foreground the tube train makes for West Ruislip.

26th July 1961

5   The location is Fenny Compton and shows in the foreground the track of the former Stratford-upon-Avon and Midland Junction Railway looking towards Woodford Halse. No 6029 **King Edward VIII** has just slowed for a P. W. restriction with the down *Cambrian Coast Express.*

29th July 1961

6   I had a few minutes to spare in Huddersfield one day and caught these two coming into the station with mainly E.R. stock. 2-6-2 tank No 42414 pilots 8F No 48265.

23rd August 1961

7   On the way home, and after passing Buxton, I came to Parsley Hay on the former Ashbourne line. Ex L.N.W.R. G2a 0-8-0 No 49391 leaves the station for Buxton. This delightful spot today is preserved for country walking and cycling.

▽

23rd August 1961

49291

8 Nearer home at Leamington Spa there was an evening freight working which came through from Banbury and was always headed by a Midland Region engine. At that time a small industrial estate was being built and it was possible to climb on to the roof tops and, in this case, see No 46118 **Royal Welch Fusilier** gently easing forward as the driver waited for the signals to clear.

31st August 1961

9 A dirty locomotive with maroon coaches on a misty morning might not seem to make a good picture. However railways often looked like this and I expect the awaiting passengers at Princes Risborough would not be really interested providing B1 No 61234 reached Nottingham on time.

2nd September 1961

10 Back to the industrial estate at Leamington Spa to see the *Inter-City* leave on its way to London double headed by No 7026 **Tenby Castle** and No 5032 **Usk Castle**. The bricklayer at least appreciates the sight and sound!

22nd September 1961

11 It must be Kings Cross and Deltic No D 9011 **The Royal Northumberland Fusiliers** just one month old poses beside Gresley A4 Pacific whose name and number I am sure you can read!

▽

25th September 1961

ENQUIRIES
SEAT & SLEEPER
RESERVATIONS
TICKET OFFICE
LADIES ROOM
TELEPHONES
NEWS OF THE WORLD
PLATFORMS
DOMINION OF NEW ZEALAND
D9011

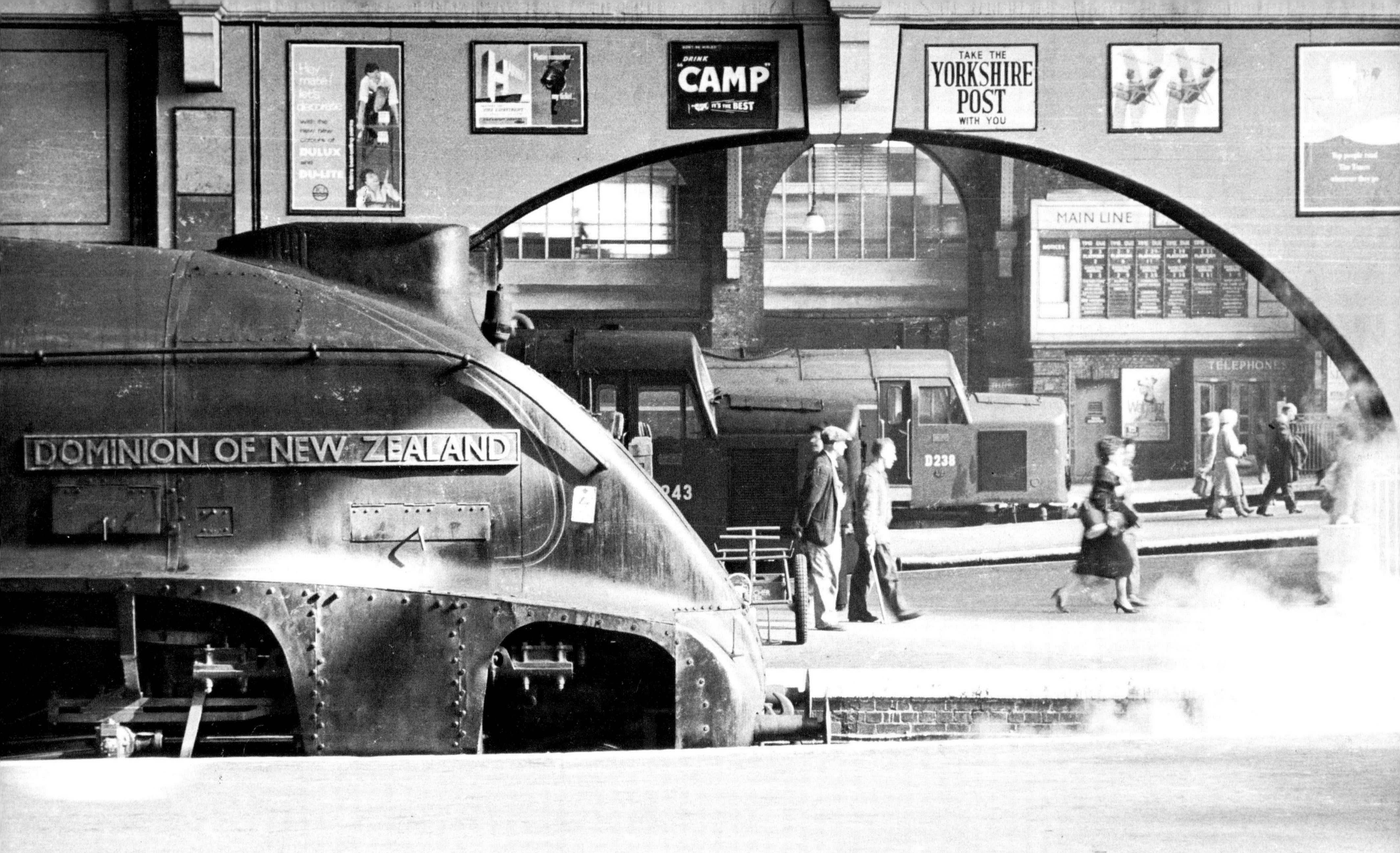

12   Just to give prominence to the steam world in face of the diesel invasion, here is another picture taken from the west side of the station but the attraction is of course the human interest and the advertising.

25th September 1961

13 The Pullman coach carries the board 'Birmingham Pullman' and No 6020 **King Henry IV** reaches the end of its journey with the morning train from the Midlands to Paddington.

25th September 1961

14   On the Merionethshire Coast at Towyn a B.R. Standard Class 2-6-2 Tank Engine No 82006 leaves for Machynlleth with a local train from Pwllheli. Note the simple layout of the yard and the track on the left with concrete supports for each chair.

30th September 1961

15   With a Crewe North Shed plate in evidence and looking very clean I am sure 2-6-0 No 78030 has recently been through the works. The locomotive is acting as station pilot at Crewe and is reversing through the station.

4th November 1961

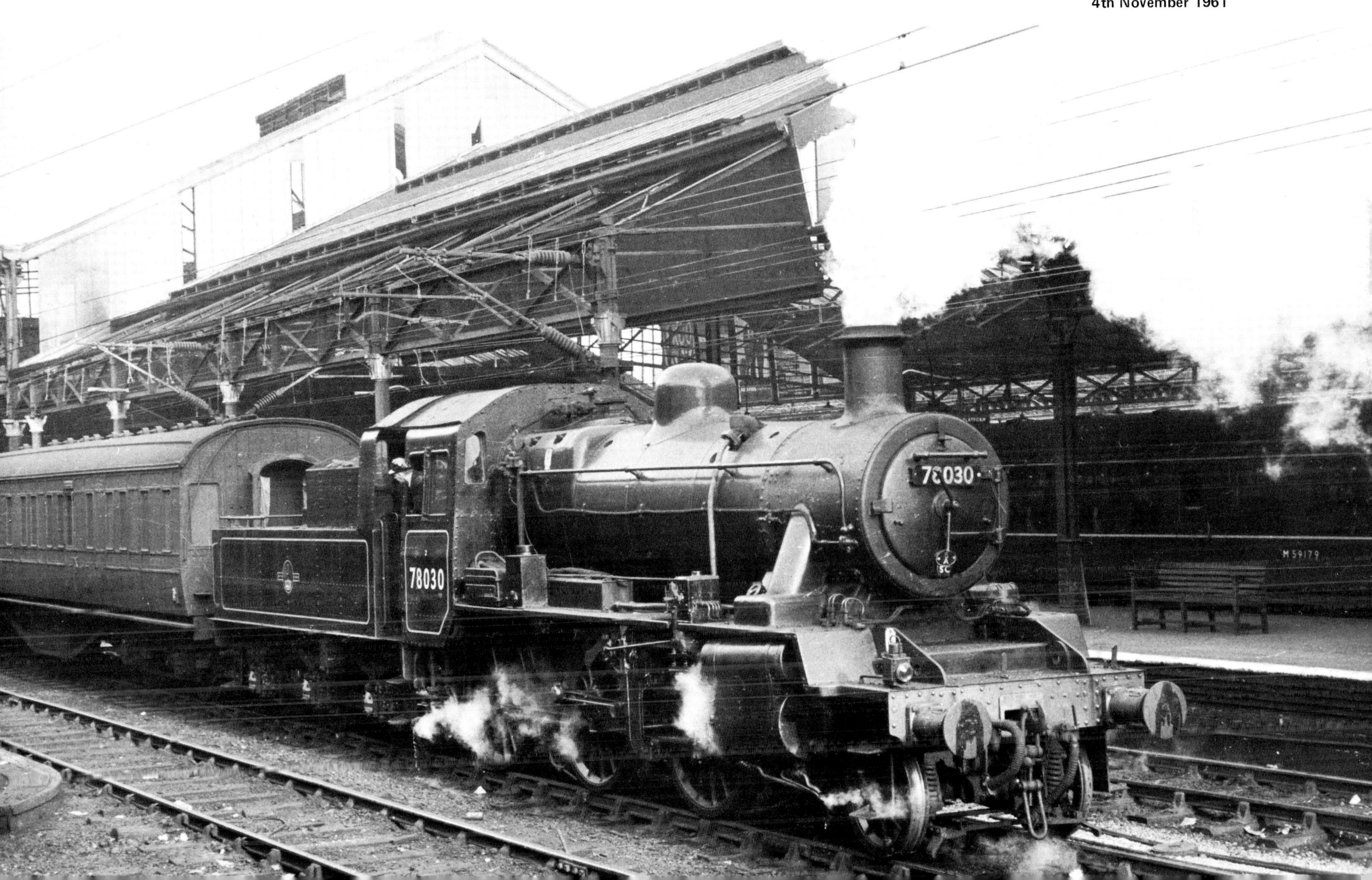

△

16   At the north end of the station the local enthusiasts are watching the arrival of No 46154 **The Hussar** with a train from Chester.

4th November 1961

17   It is good to be reminded of the signalling at Leamington Spa as it is all colour light today. No 6000 **King George V** awaits the green flag with the down *Cambrian Coast Express.*

11th November 1961

Z 3 0
7014

18   The small frame in front of the fogman's hut is used for placing the detonators on the down line under the centre of the leading coach. No 7014 **Caerhays Castle** breasts the top of Hatton Bank with a football special.

17th February 1962

19   Steam and Diesel at Kings Cross with the station staff cleaning carriage windows. 'Britannia' Pacific No 70038 **Robin Hood** has just arrived from Cleethorpes and stands in a ray of sunshine with the arch of the station framing the picture.

14th March 1962

67793
1A30

20   I failed to record the name of the Deltic about to leave Kings Cross but the enthusiast seems to be looking it up in his book. Class L1 2-6-4T No 67793 makes a nice contrast alongside.

14th March 1962

21   No 5991 **Gresham Hall** passes through Swindon station with a westbound freight. The photograph makes an interesting comparison with the very changed scene of today.

31st March 1962

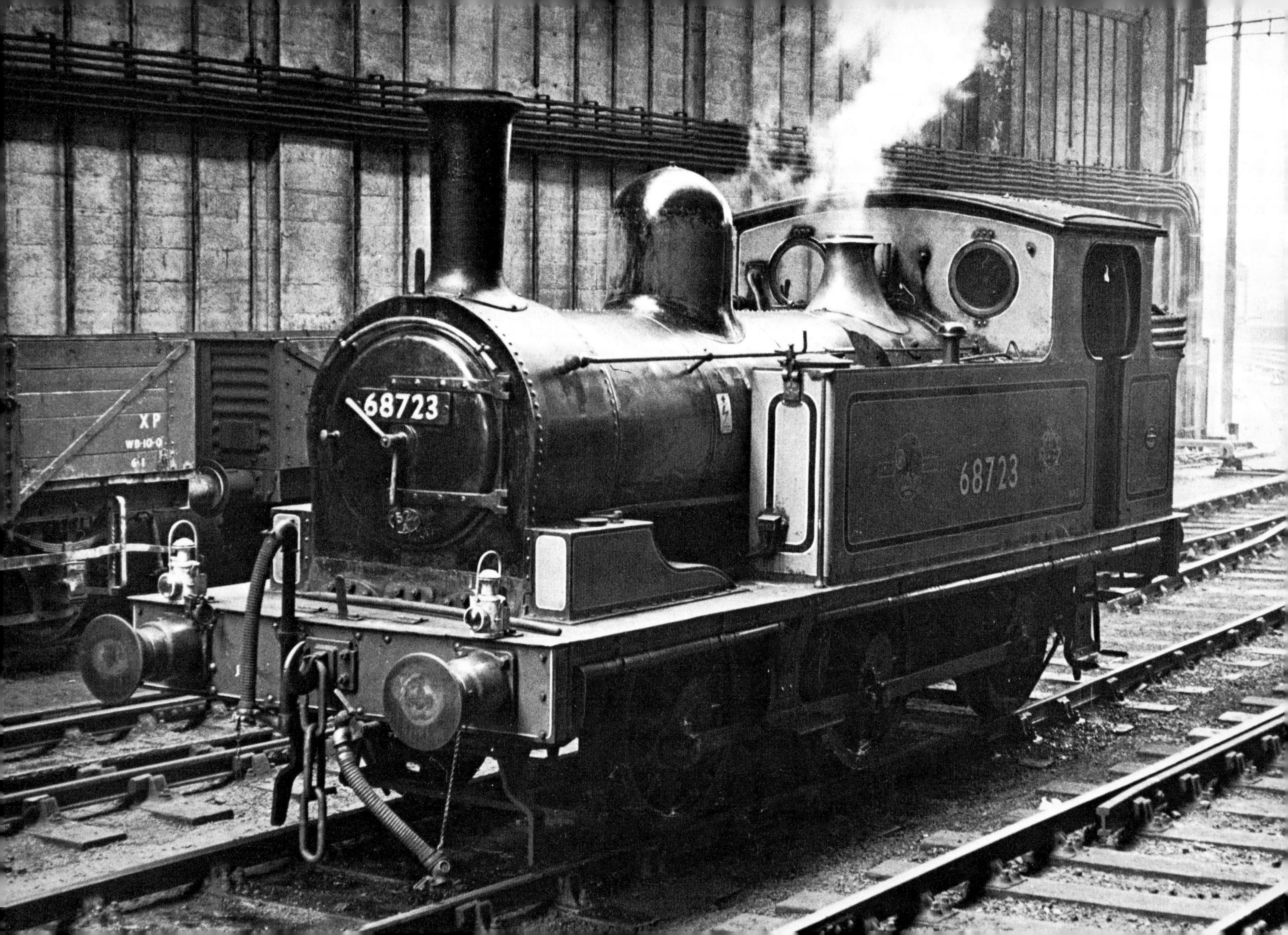

22 A quick visit to Newcastle by train produced this picture taken out of the carriage window as the southbound journey commenced. Class J72 0-6-0 tank engine No 68723 acts as station pilot and is painted in North Eastern livery.

20th April 1962

23 *The Aberdeen Flyer* was a special train from Kings Cross to Aberdeen and back down the west coast to Euston. Running over two hours late, due to electrification of the line, No 46200 **The Princess Royal** leaves Rugby with the familiar wireless masts in the background.

3rd June 1962

24 Now safely in preservation at Dinting No 45596 **Bahamas** heads north on the West Coast main line near Cranberry, north of Stafford. The wires are up but electric haulage had not yet commenced.

9th June 1962

25 In the opposite direction and travelling very fast, 'Britannia' Pacific No 70046 **Anzac** has the driver looking very carefully from the cab window.

▽

9th June 1962

1 0 1 1
ANZAC
70046

26   In the afternoon I moved north to Whitmore and saw No 71000 **Duke of Gloucester** coming round the curve from Crewe. This is the engine now being restored at Loughborough. Note the Caprotti valve gear.

9th June 1962

27   On the water troughs now, and unnamed 'Britannia' Pacific No 70047 overfills its tender quite surprisingly as it is near the commencement of the pick up.

▽

9th June 1962

28 No 46240 **City of Coventry** passes the sight of the former station at Whitmore and the steam coming from the rear of the tender shows that the coal pusher is in operation. A fine looking locomotive travelling at speed.

9th June 1962

29 Back to Swindon again with a view at the west end of the station as No 6931 **Aldborough Hall** is inspected by crowds of engine spotters on all platforms. The works is of course in the background.

▽

13th June 1962

30 While the Euston–Crewe electrification was being carried out Sunday trains came through Leamington Avenue station on various occasions. *The Ulster Express* with No 46208 **Princess Helena Victoria** passes on its way north and the W.R. station is in the background.

1st July 1962

31 I much enjoyed the occasional visit to Kings Cross as there was a total mix of Steam and Diesel. 'Britannia' Pacific No 70038 **Robin Hood** eases its train into the station.

▽

18th July 1962

70038

CAMP
"COS IT'S THE BEST"
Shapes
You can
rely on
FOXHUNTER
60134
1A09

△

32 The mixture becomes more apparent down at the buffer stops with the diesel even having brackets above the buffers for taking oil lamps!

18th July 1962

33 A departure with No 60119 **Patrick Stirling** just about to slip violently but too late for my camera.

18th July 1962

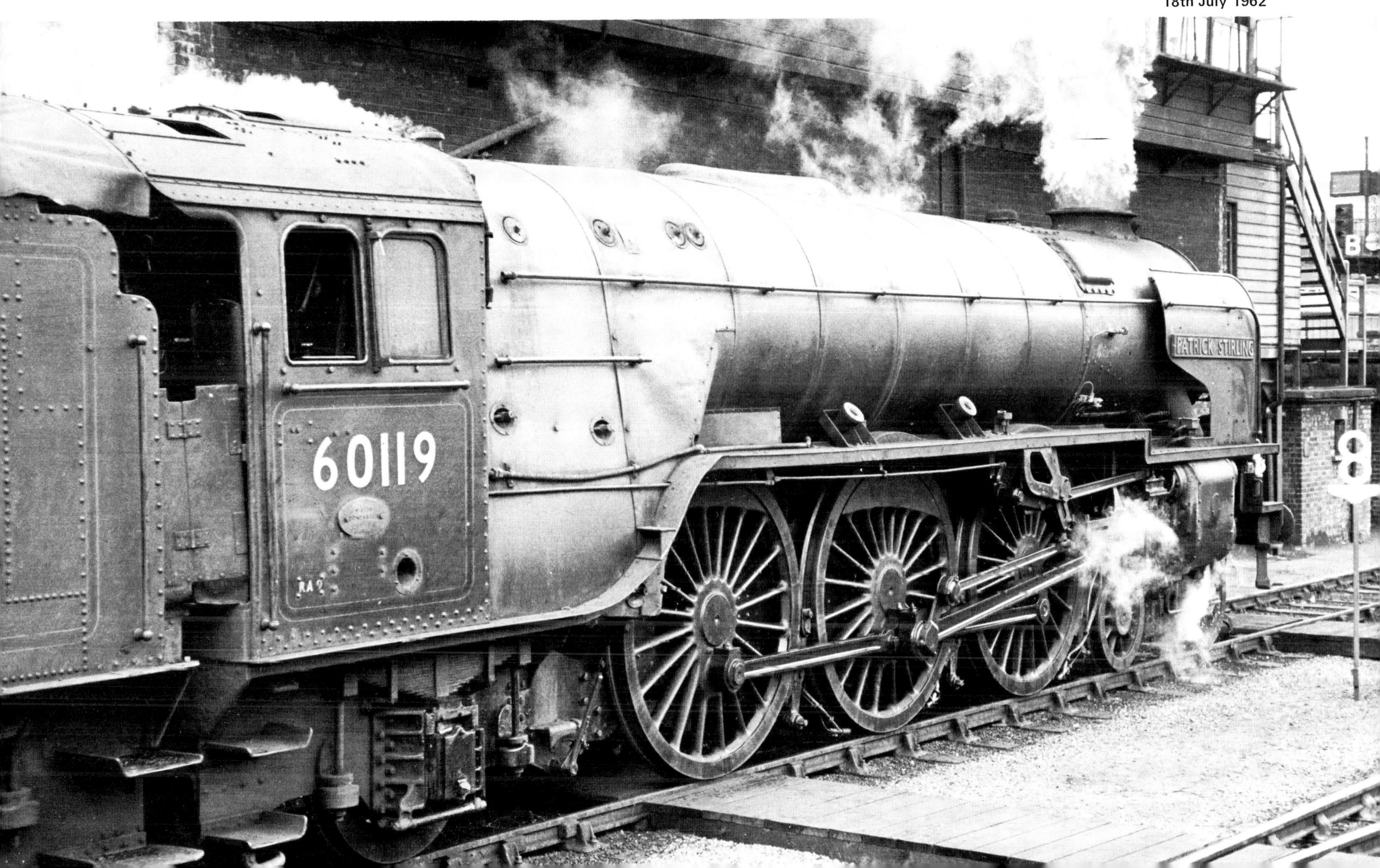

60029
WOODCOCK
60029
A·4

34 The driver of No 60029 **Woodcock** moves slowly down to the coaches as the fireman prepares to couple up having first removed the lamp which he has placed on the ground.

18th July 1962

35 The heap of coal on the tender looks as if it is outside the loading gauge. The diesel-hauled express has a set of Pullman cars with one of the conductors leaning out of the first coach.

18th July 1962

36 An unusual combination at the arrival side of Paddington Station with
No D854 **Tiger** leading No 4932 **Hatherton Hall**. Up in Brunel's roof tar-
paulins hang to protect the passengers from the painters!

18th July 1962

37 The next set of pictures were taken around Southampton during the
summer timetable. No 34059 **Sir Archibald Sinclair** awaits departure
with S15 Class No 30508 in the background.

▽

25th August 1962

SIR ARCHIBALD SINCLAIR
7P 5FA
34059

38   The train number on the smokebox has covered the locomotive number so I cannot tell you which one it is. Note the design of the station lamp brackets.

25th August 1962

39   This is the classic view at Southampton showing the signal gantry and docks in the background. North Eastern coaches abound as they approach the station behind No 34041 **Wilton**.

▽

25th August 1962

40   The sunlight near the coast is always brilliant and No 34050 **Royal Observer Corps** glistens as it departs for Bournemouth.

25th August 1962

41   Nos 41329 and 82014 approach Totton with an oil tanker train from the Fawley Refinery. Note the two wagons inserted to reduce any fire risk from the locomotives, and I wonder if the drivers are having an interesting conversation.

25th August 1962

42 In the afternoon the return working for Waterloo started to appear and this one has come up from Lymington with passengers from the Isle of Wight. 'Schools' Class No 30935 **Sevenoaks** emerges from under the A35.

25th August 1962

43 Passing Redbridge signal box is another up express from Bournemouth with No 34032 **Camelford** in charge. Note the small shed with engine off duty for the weekend.

▽

25th August 1962

34032
385
30
40

44 Taken from the same footbridge but showing a train coming in from the Salisbury line and most likely going to Brighton. No 34055 **Fighter Pilot** emits a healthy heat haze in front of the cottages.

25th August 1962

45 Just to the west of Southampton station the line swings round to the north west and No 34102 **Lapford** passes a well cared for Austin Seven standing in the brilliant sunshine.

▽ **25th August 1962**

34102
039

46 This was the one I had been waiting for all day and for once the sun shone. The picture of this magnificent sight tells all and I only need to mention that the locomotive is No 35030 **Elder Dempster Lines.**

25th August 1962

47 Most trains took water at Southampton and there was time for me to run back to the station and see the *Bournemouth Belle* having the tender refilled. In the foreground is No 34006 **Bude** and a delightful collection of spotters.

▽

25th August 1962

SOUTHAMPTON
CENTRAL
34006
34006
301
36
35030
33

48 Perhaps three pictures of the same train are rather too many but I could not resist this one of the departure with a close up of the first car with passengers sitting at their tables. Note the spectators above the tunnel mouth.

25th August 1962

49 Most steam enthusiasts enjoy the sight of a paddle steamer and this one was built for the Southern Railway in 1937. Here it is arriving off Ryde Pier Head with some holidaymakers from Southsea.

August 1962

SANDOWN

32661

50 This could be called a 'conversation piece' at Hayling Island Station. Note the size of 'Terrier' Class No 32661 compared with the coach, and the island platform with gas lighting.

27th August 1962

51 Langstone Bridge, passed shortly after leaving Havant, was an all timber affair and here the 'Terrier' is on its way south. Notice the road bridge in the background.

27th August 1962

52   The two Class N Moguls Nos 31871 and 31868 give a Southern Region atmosphere to this scene at Reading General. No 5058 **Earl of Clancarty** passes through with a returning train of milk wagons.

14th September 1962

53   This was the year when the Western diesels were introduced in large numbers and here we see No D1005 **Western Venturer** climbing past Gresford Colliery with a Birkenhead to Paddington train, leaving Chester at 09.15.

29th September 1962

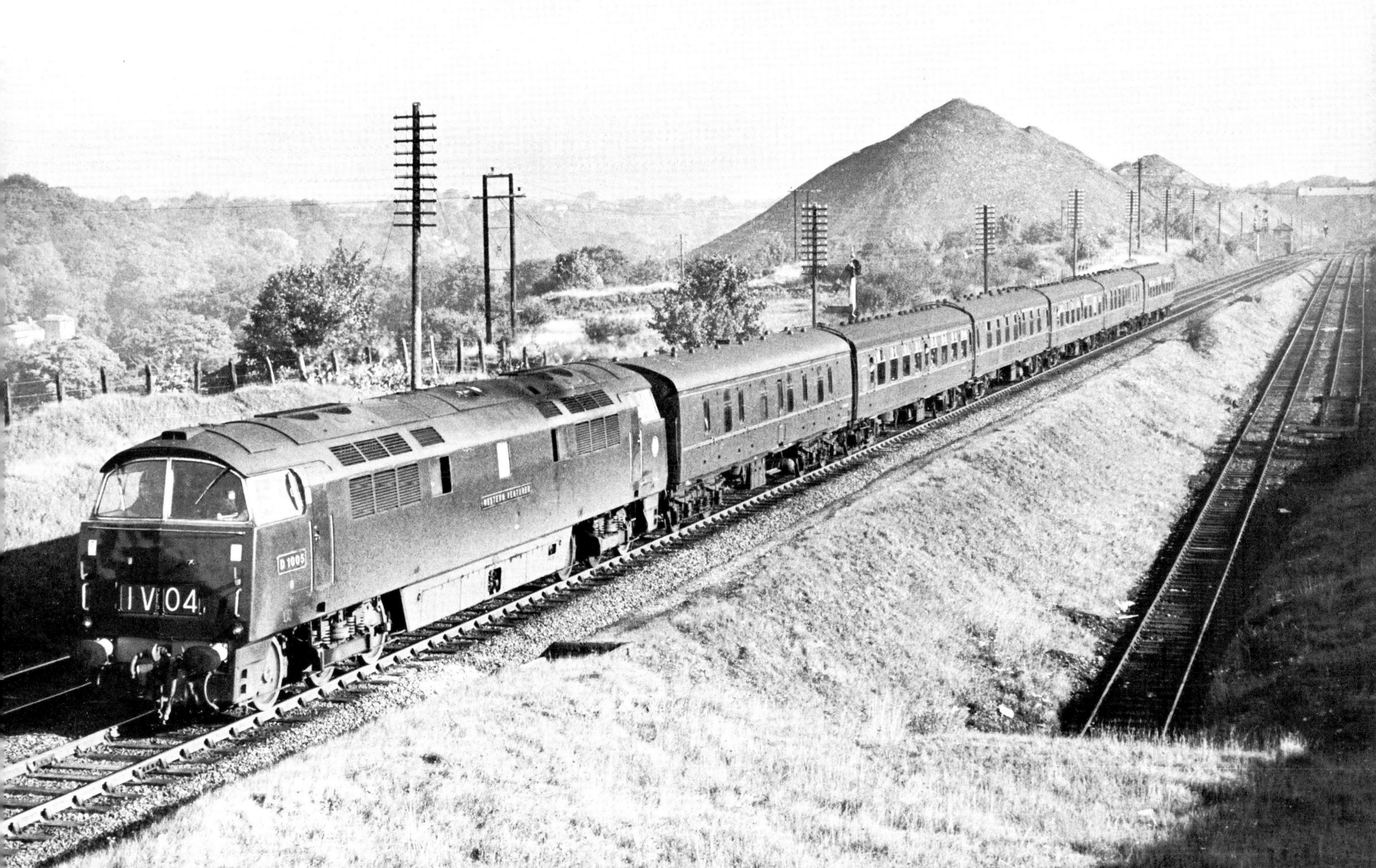

WESTERN VENTURER
D 1005
1V 04

45268
BRITISH RAILWAYS

54 A clean Class 5 No 45268 in the down platform at Leamington Spa.
The present line to Coventry swings to the right just beyond the signal
box.

20th October 1962

55 A few weeks later another Class 5 No 44712 is in trouble at the other
end of the station with a steam crane preparing to lift the front end of
the locomotive and replace it on the track.

18th November 1962

56   Now we move on to 1963 when No 4472 **Flying Scotsman** had been purchased for preservation and was making its first run in L.N.E.R. livery. A terrible day but it makes an impressive sight climbing towards Ruabon with the Festiniog Railway Preservation Society Special.

20th April 1963

57   In the afternoon the locomotive worked light engine to Shrewsbury and here it is crossing the River Dee.

20th April 1963

58 On arrival at Shrewsbury **Flying Scotsman** was serviced and came onto the turntable. The return working left in the early hours of Sunday morning for Paddington.

20 April 1963

59 Southampton Football Club were playing in Birmingham and no less than thirteen special trains conveyed the supporters to Birmingham. All but one had S.R. engines and the majority climbed Hatton Bank in the morning. Here is No 34045 **Ottery St. Mary** at the location where many enthusiasts watch the special steam trains today.

27th April 1963

△

60 In the afternoon there seemed more S.R. engines on Tyseley shed than G.W. and here No 34046 **Braunton** stands beside No 34039 **Boscastle** with a very subdued No 7929 **Wyke Hall** to the right of the picture.

27th April 1963

61 The following day No 6018 **King Henry VI** made the last run of the class having been withdrawn the previous autumn. Having attained a maximum speed of 92 m.p.h. near Denham the engine takes a rest on Swindon Shed amid Hymek hydraulic diesels, before returning to the Midlands.

28th April 1963

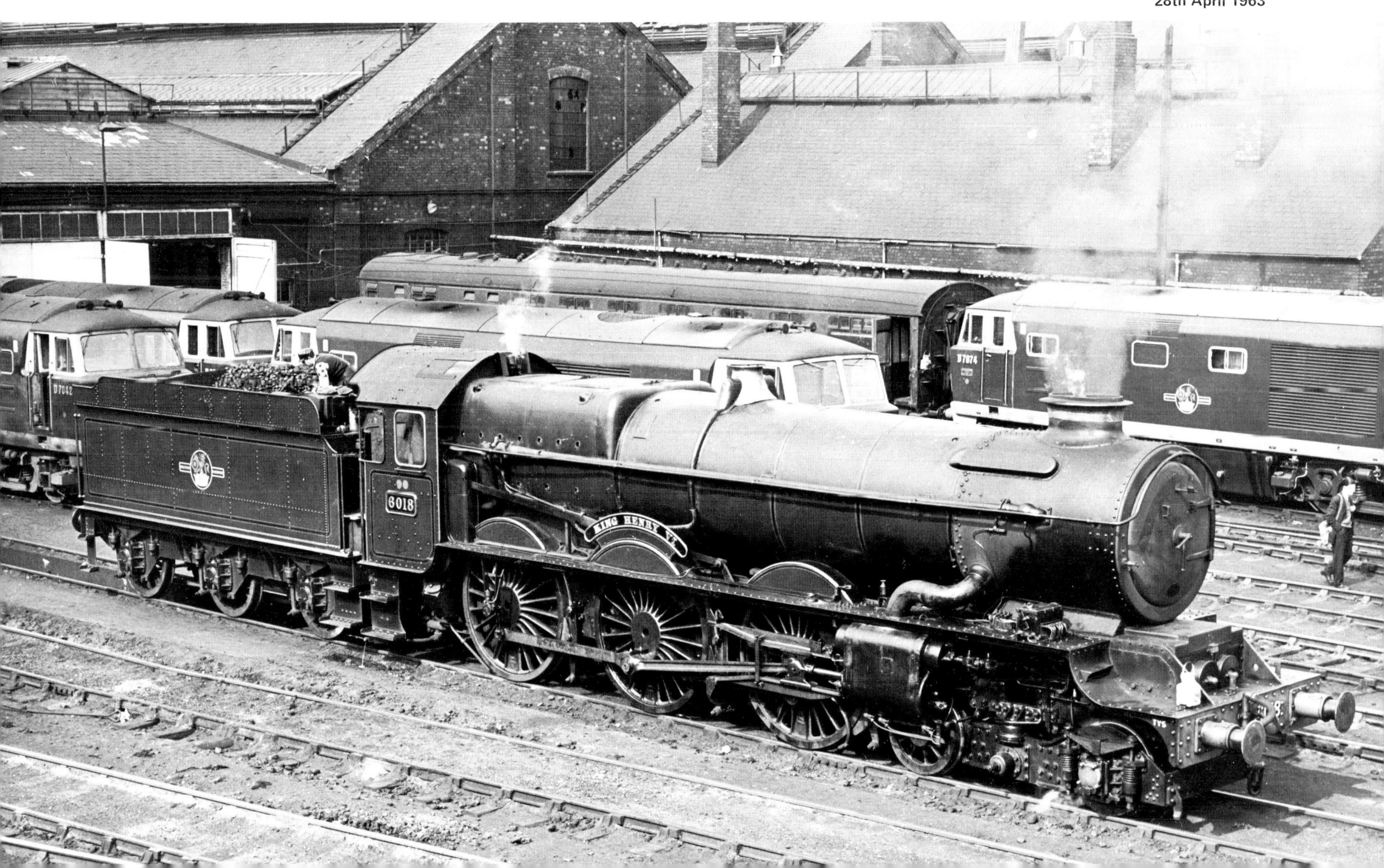

S·L·S
SPECIAL
777
6018

△

62   The route back to Birmingham was through Oxford and I wonder if this was the first occasion that a 'King' had worked through that city.

28th April 1963

63   Cup Final day at Wembley brought a number of Special trains down the Great Central route. Class 5 No 45334 is about to enter Catesby Tunnel near Charwelton.

25th May 1963

1X55
45626
45626

△

64   At the other end of the Tunnel No 45626 **Seychelles** hurries through
the cutting which is derelict and empty today.
          25th May 1963

65   As this was the last main line built out of London the date on the
tunnel mouth 1897 seems very modern. Class 9F No 92229 heads north
for Rugby.
          25th May 1963

△

66 Just to the south of Woodford Halse is a triangle connecting up with the S.M.J.R. and between the football specials an 8F No 48385 passes through with No 48002 in the background.

25th May 1963

67 The last special was headed by No 45598 **Basutoland** and is passing under the line from Stratford-upon-Avon to Blisworth.

25th May 1963

68   Further north at Staverton Road signal box I waited to see this **up** freight train hauled by 9F No 92072.

25th May 1963

69   An Autumn special train found No 45552 **Silver Jubilee** climbing the Lickey Incline with a 9F banker at the rear. The smoke effect was quite remarkable and the train went up to Birmingham and straight back again.

▽

12th October 1963

45676

70 A service train runs into Barnt Green station behind No 45676 **Codrington** under the fine set of signals one of which has a wooden post.

12th October 1963

71 Another set of fine signals of L.N.W.R. origin are a well known feature of Chester Station. Class 5 No 45352 passes Chester No 4 Signal Box with a freight train from the Holyhead main line.

2nd November 1963

73040
CHESTER

72　The trains from Shrewsbury to Chester were often hauled by B.R. Standard locomotives and in this case Class 5 No 73040 comes into the arrival Bay.

2nd November 1963

73　The Stephenson Locomotive Society ran a railtour from Birmingham to Shrewsbury, Newport, Severn Tunnel Junction, Swindon and back to Birmingham. Here the train is seen from the carriage window slowly negotiating the west curve at Shrewsbury.

26th April 1964

S·L·S
SPECIAL
4073

74 The locomotive for the tour was No 4079 **Pendennis Castle** and here the train is shortly to depart from Hereford having stopped for the 650 passengers to inspect Barton Shed.

26th April 1964

75 Southampton again with the fireman off No 34009 **Lyme Regis** either shouting to the driver to turn off the water or perhaps he is gazing at some attractive passenger on one of the other platforms!

6th June 1964

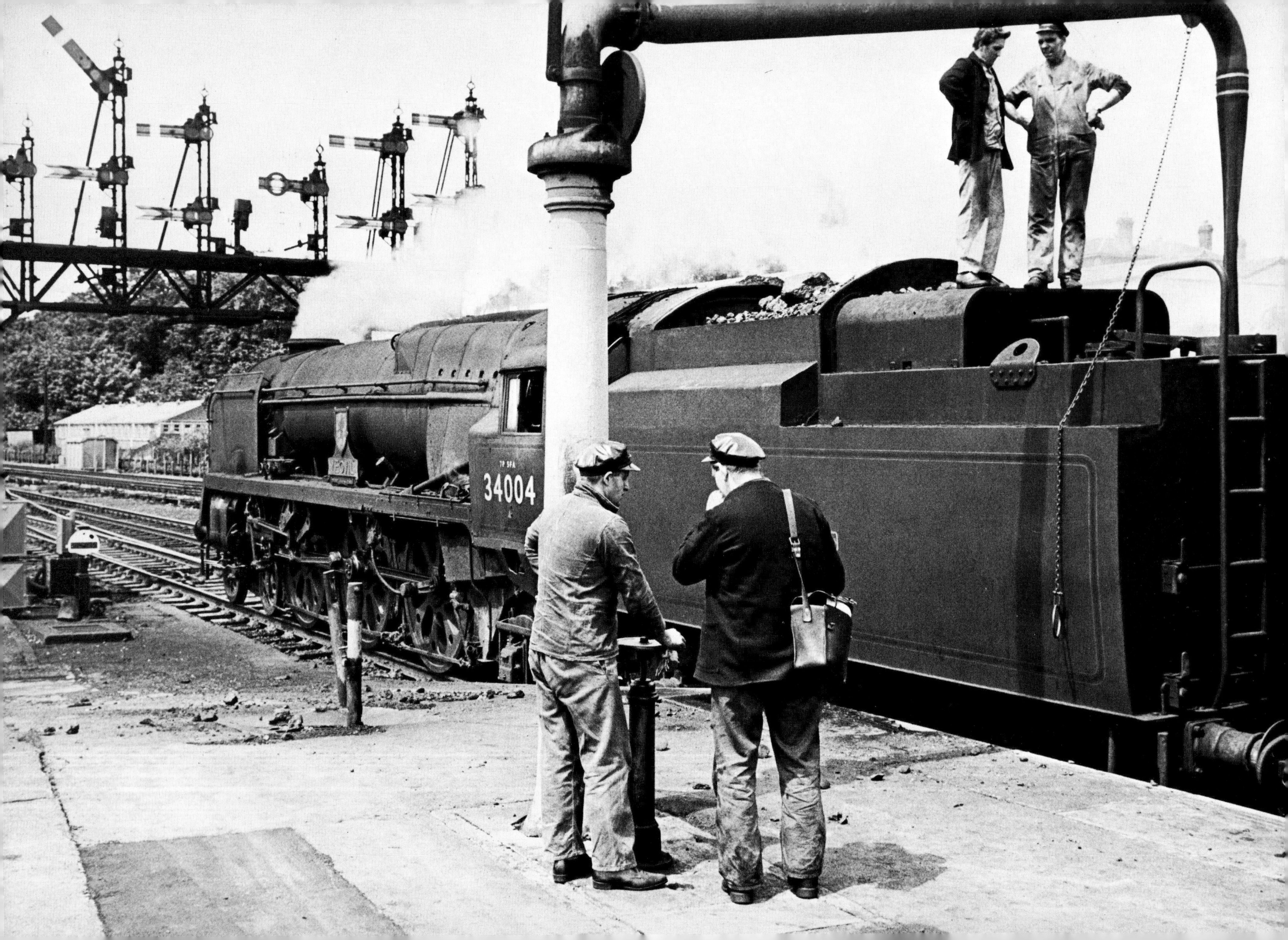

7P 5FA
34004
L

76 Another 'conversation piece' this time at Southampton where a change of crew is taking place and refilling the tender provides time for both sets of men to exchange views on the mechanical state of No 34004 **Yeovil**.

6th June 1964

77 The Royal Train is in the exchange sidings at Leamington Spa conveying the Queen Mother from Kenilworth to Stratford-upon-Avon. This required a change of direction and another Class 5 is waiting to take over from No 45322.

11th July 1964

78   This departure from Aberystwyth on the Vale of Rheidol Railway shows No 9 **Prince of Wales** running along the old route past the engine sheds to be seen just above the fourth coach.

July 1964

79   My first and only visit to Eastleigh Works took place to coincide with a Warwickshire Railway Society special train from Birmingham behind No 4472 **Flying Scotsman**.

Two 'West Country' Pacifics stand in the sun outside the shed

16th August 1964

80 Resplendent in a new coat of paint after overhaul in the works 'Terrier' tank No 32650 makes a stark contrast with the other larger engines. Fortunately it is now preserved on the Kent and East Sussex Railway.
16th August 1964

81 Within the works 'Merchant Navy' No 35012 **United States Lines** is receiving attention to the valve gear. Note the connecting rods lying on the floor.

16th August 1964

35012
35012
MERCHANT NAVY CLASS
UNITED STATES LINES

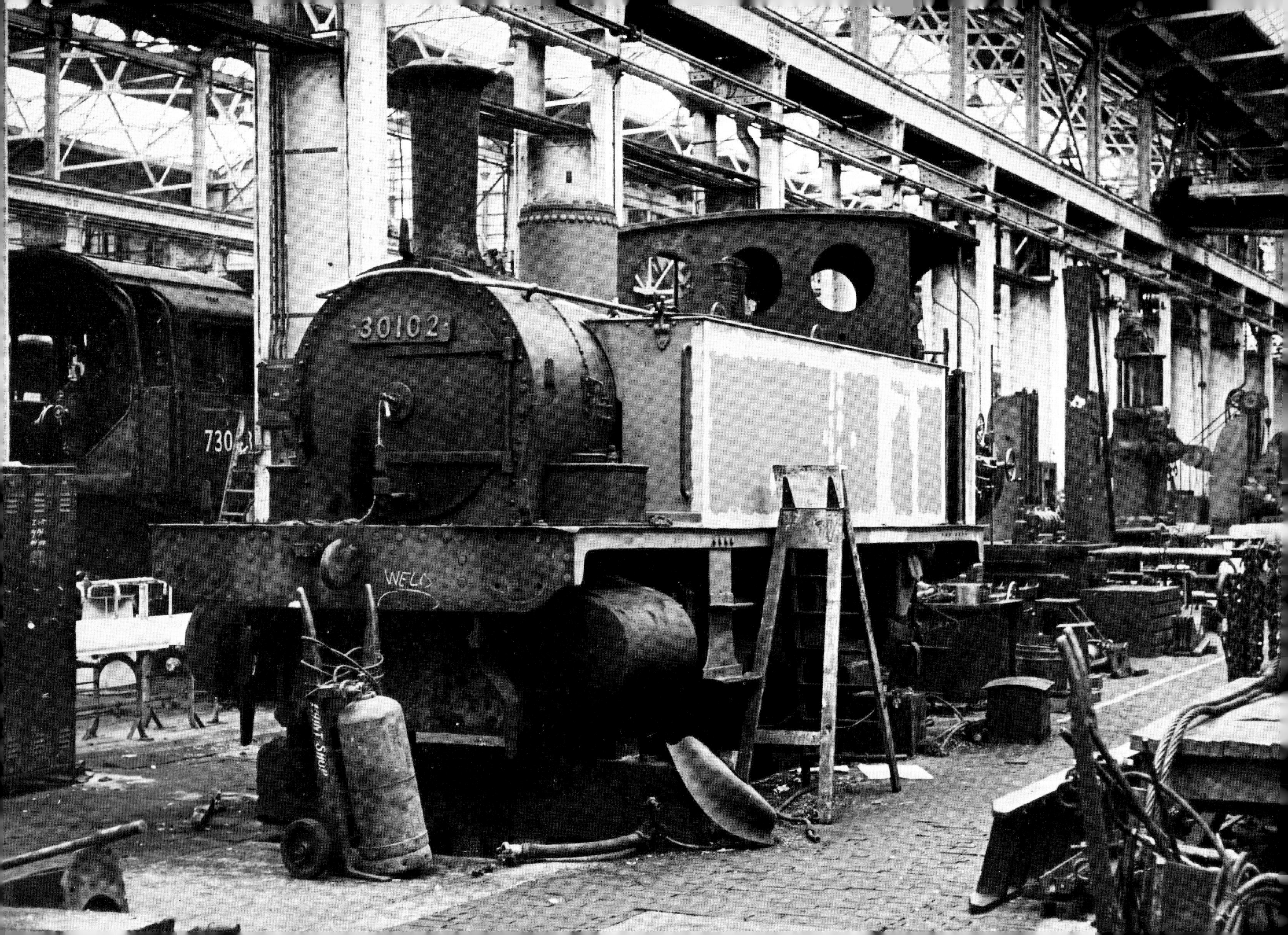

30102
730
WELD
PAINT SHOP

△

82 Another locomotive now in preservation at Bressingham Hall in Norfolk. Class B4 0-4-0T No 30102 is sitting quietly on two enormous timbers surrounded by the usual workshop bits and pieces.

16th August 1964

83 I make no excuse for including this one as it is one of my favourite shots of No 4472 **Flying Scotsman** as it leaves Leamington Spa with a special train for the Farnborough Air Display

12th September 1964

84   A few days later was the annual Stephenson Locomotive Society trip to Swindon. In this case it was hauled by the last 'County' Class locomotive No 1011 **County of Chester** seen here at the east end of Swindon station.

20th September 1964

85   Down at the locomotive shed were two engines now safely in preservation. 9F No 92203 operates on the East Somerset Railway and No 7808 **Cookham Manor** is part of the collection at Didcot. On the left may be seen the buffers of M7 0-4-4T No 30667.

▽

20th September 1964

92203
7808
D7087

86   Already destined for preservation No 4555 stands outside the Shed at Croes Newydd ready to take a special to Towyn.

26th September 1964

87   The shed lies on a triangle and here is an empty coal train taking the route to Brymbo coal mine. The locomotive 8F No 48090 passes by two A.T.C. test ramps in the yard.

26th September 1964

88 The special train for the Talyllyn Preservation Society has now left Ruabon and takes the line for Llangollen, Corwen, Dolgellau and Barmouth. The 'Manor' Class 4-6-0 No 7827 **Lydham Manor** is now in preservation on the Torbay Steam Railway.

26th September 1964

89 On my way to Neston I called in at Mold Junction Shed and found this trio resting peacefully in the late Autumn sunshine.

26th September 1964

90 'A last train' to run on the Stratford-upon-Avon and Midland Junction Railway was organised by the Stephenson Locomotive Society from Birmingham to Woodford Halse and return. In the outward direction 4F No 44188 and restored pannier tank No 6435 have just passed under the aqueduct at Bearley.

24th April 1965

91 The pannier tank only went as far as Stratford-upon-Avon and in this picture the 4F No 44188 is returning in the afternoon passing Byfield station.

▽

24th April 1965

S·L·S
SPECIAL
44188
BESCOT
44188

S·L·S
SPECIAL
·35017·
SPL
11
7C 17

92 Another S.L.S. special *The Bulleid Pacific Rail Tour* ran from Birmingham to Exeter outward via Basingstoke and return through Westbury. No 35017 **Belgian Marine** stands at Exeter Central taking on water. It worked the leg from Salisbury to Westbury.

23rd May 1965

93 The last scheduled steam hauled service from Paddington ran to Banbury. No 7029 **Clun Castle** did the honours and here it is backing down to Banbury Shed with a 'Western' Class diesel hydraulic speeding past without stopping at the station.

11th June 1965

94   To end the volume, I have included this picture of a 9F No 92013 passing Charwelton village with a freight for the North Midlands. The water troughs are visible in the background—a desolate scene today.

Date unknown